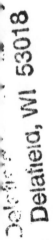

Delafield, WI 53018

CYCLING

WRITTEN BY GEORGE JENKINS

ROURKE CORPORATION, INC.
VERO BEACH, FLORIDA 32964

PRO-AM
SPORTS

The Rourke Corporation, Inc.
P.O. Box 3328, Vero Beach, FL 32964

Jenkins, George H., 1950-
        Cycling / George Jenkins.
            p.   cm. — (Pro-am sports)
        Includes bibliographical references (p. 46).
        ISBN 0-86593-350-2
        1. Cycling. I. Title. II. Series.
    GV1041.J46 1993
    796.6—dc20   93-36545
                                                    CIP
                                                     AC

Cover photograph: Rich Cruse
Interior Photographs:
Allsport 4; 9 (Pascal Rondeau); 33 (Mike Powell);
        44 (David Cannon)
American Bicycle Association 5, 6, 10, 14, 16, 18, 19,
        21, 23
Bureau of Land Management, 28
Rich Cruse 12, 15, 25, 26, 27, 30, 31, 35, 36, 38, 40, 43
Stock Montage, Inc., 8

Series Editor: Gregory Lee
Book design and production:
        The Creative Spark, San Clemente, CA

Printed in the USA

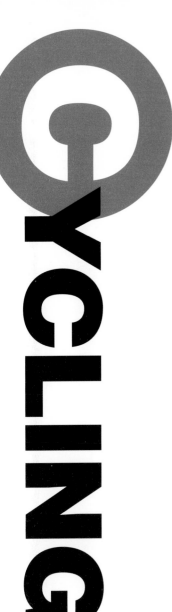

CYCLING

Fun, fitness, and competition. The most popular type of transportation in the world—cycling—has it all.

CONTENTS

HOT TIP:

Have you ever heard of a bicycle with no brakes? *Turn to page 41.*

Bicycling is one of the simplest and most enjoyable activities we learn at an early age—and can enjoy for a lifetime.

Cycling Thrills

CHAPTER ONE

Do you remember the first time you managed to ride a two-wheel bicycle on your own without someone holding you up? That sensation of freedom is one of the first and best experiences you remember about growing up. No one really remembers when they first learned to walk, but practically everyone remembers when they learned to ride.

Bicycles are pure enjoyment, and we never seem to outgrow them. Although they are the first transportation of youth, millions of people keep enjoying bicycles long after they begin driving automobiles. Because they're so much fun, it's no surprise that bicycles have become popular for racing. We start by racing our friends to the end of a street, or all the way to school. In the past 20 years kids developed a style of racing that imitated the popular adult style of motorcycle racing called moto-cross.

When the moto begins, every rider is on his own.

Now youths all over North America race in *motos*—individual sprints against other bicycle riders, bouncing and swerving around a bumpy track for a prize. What is it like to compete in a bicycle moto-cross race?

When your moto is called, you and the rest of the riders in your heat line up at the starting point. You adjust your helmet and goggles, and position your right pedal so that it is in the high position. Your arms tense slightly as you grip the handlebars and take one quick glance at the other riders around you. Then you stare straight ahead and prepare to sprint.

Table-tops are just one of several obstacles built into the BMX racing course.

The flag drops. Your right foot pushes hard down on the high pedal for a power start. The race will be short and fast, and you know a fast kickoff will make the difference between winning and losing. The start is inclined, and each rider does his best to break from the rest of the pack before reaching the first speed bumps. Two bumps face the racers before they reach the first turn to the left. Each rider tries to crowd the turn, not allowing any rider behind them to pass.

After the turn you face the first incline with a pair of table tops at the top of the climb. These are short, flat rises meant to increase the difficulty of your sprint. Next comes the second left-hand turn leading to the first straightaway. Throughout the entire race you concentrate on making your rear wheel turn as fast as possible to increase speed.

At the end of the straightaway, you face another climb to a step-up jump at the top. As you descend, coming fast is the third left-hand turn. You ride the berm in a hard fast turn then plunge into a series of whoop-de-dos. You struggle to control your bike as you pitch up and down, doing your best to keep driving as fast as possible. Your stomach, knees, and spine feel the bounces as you push harder through these churning mounds. The crowd roars with excitement as each rider leaps off the mounds and gets air.

The finish is near as you enter the first right-hand turn and power up the third incline which drops off immediately into the final right-hand turn. Facing you is the straightaway, with a drop off just before the finish line. You've done everything just right, made the right moves at the crucial places, and find yourself zooming across the finish line the winner! The race is over in less than 40 seconds. Depending upon your placement in this moto, you collect points, may ride in the next moto, and possibly win a trophy.

The world of bicycle moto-cross or BMX racing is just one type of bicycling you'll find causing excitement among kids, teenagers, and adults all over North America. Bicycling in all its forms is one of the most popular activities in the world. People use bicycles for transportation as well as competition and sport, and bikes are a never-ending source of good exercise and downright fun. Let's explore a little further this world of bicycling.

A Little History

Bicycles have been around since ancient times—at least, historians think so. Egyptian hieroglyphics and sculptures by other ancient peoples seem to show individuals riding on long sticks clearly connected to two wheels. Roman paintings on the walls of the ill-fated city of Pompeii portray men in togas enjoying two-wheelers. These Romans knew about steel, bronze, and copper, because they had a flourishing weapons industry. It's possible that they could have re-invented the bicycle long after the ancient Egyptians.

Unfortunately, those contraptions shown in ancient art will likely remain a mystery, because no ancient bicycle has ever been found by archaeologists. Yet these ancients clearly had the idea of what a bicycle looked like and how it could be used.

The bicycle made its next appearance in the sketchbooks of that Renaissance genius, Leonardo da Vinci. Many of our modern inventions were actually conceived of by this incredible man long before they were finally made. For example, he described and drew tanks, helicopters, submarines, and a chain-driven vehicle that looks suspiciously like a bicycle. His drawings were complete, including details of the chain mechanism!

The bicycle didn't reappear in modern times until 1690 when a French woodworker, Elie Richard, drafted plans for an elementary two-wheeler. Years

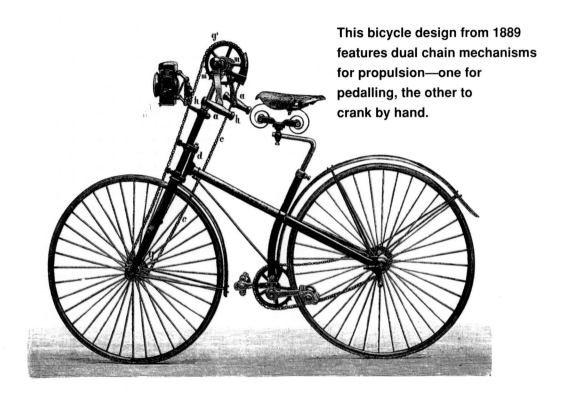

This bicycle design from 1889 features dual chain mechanisms for propulsion—one for pedalling, the other to crank by hand.

later a French engineer named Jacques Azanam built a model of a two-wheeler from Richard's plans. Not until 1779 did two Frenchmen, Masurier and Blanchard, succeed in building a working bike: It was a huge wooden beam, with a wheel front and back that could not be steered. Their attempt faded into history.

Many tried and many failed to make a working bicycle in France, England, and the United States. The person credited with inventing the first truly modern bicycle was Kirkpatric Macmillan, a Scottish engineer who succeeded by building, like most successful engineers, on others' failures. He called it a *velocipede*. The first race using one was held in Paris on May 30, 1869 in the Parc de Saint-Cloud. The race was 1,200 meters long. Even then, people knew a good thing when they saw it. The race was cleverly sponsored by the French bike manufacturer, the Compagnie Parisienne de Velocipedes.

Bikes for the World

The total number of bikes around the world today probably numbers in the billions. For one thing, the bicycle is the principal form of transportation in China—home to one-quarter of the Earth's population. In fact, bicycles have

Cycling is popular throughout the world. In fact, it is the most common form of transportation in many countries.

been and remain to this day the main transportation device on the globe. In 1992 alone, world bicycle production outnumbered automobile production by three-to-one. While less developed nations like China, India, and others depend almost exclusively on bicycles for their daily transportation needs, in North America and other Western nations the bike is used mostly for exercise and sport.

Thousands of amateur American and European bike lovers participate in bicycle sports activities throughout the year. The most popular of these are road and track racing, off road riding and racing, and bicycle moto-cross. Many riders are fortunate to excel as amateurs and, due to their great riding skills, may find themselves sponsored by a bicycle manufacturer and pedaled into the world of the professional athlete. For most young people, the road to professional biking begins with bicycle moto-cross, or BMX!

Back in the 1960s, kids wanted to use their bikes for racing, just like professional moto-cross racers. The BMX bike was born.

The BMX
Breakthrough

C H A P T E R T W O

Bicycle moto-cross evolved from motorcycle moto-cross events that became popular in the U.S. after World War II. From the times when both the bicycle and the motorcycle were invented, riders have always enjoyed riding "off the road" to test their skills. As off road riding became more popular with motorcycle riders, the builders of these motor bikes began to design them to handle the rough country and still continue to run.

Young people are no different than adults, and knew from an early age that riding their bikes in the dirt was a lot of fun. Like motorcycle riders, boys and girls found that they had to practice and learn new skills to ride off road.

In the 1970s the Schwinn Bicycle Company saw that thousands of boys and girls were creating off road dirt tracks of their own on unused open spaces like vacant lots and fields. These tracks copied the race courses used by their idols—the motorcycle moto-cross racers. These sand lot race tracks were complete with jumps, turns, and obstacles, just like the motorcycle tracks.

Boys and girls across the country were calling their new sport bicycle moto-cross, or BMX for short. BMX grew in popularity among all age groups, but today it remains primarily a sport of young people.

A lot was happening in the 1970s. During this time motorcycles were never more popular, and for kids too young to drive a motorcycle, the 10-speed bike was the most popular bicycle in America. The popularity of the 10-speed was so great that manufacturers had great difficulty keeping up with demand. At one point, 10-speed bikes were being stolen at a rate of one bike for every new bike made!

The 10-speed bike, however, was not suited for off road riding or racing. Its frame, wheel rims, and tires were all wrong for the rough-and-tumble style of

Back in the '70s, riders were getting tougher with their 10-speeds, needing a stronger bike designed to take off road punishment.

BMX, and the kids knew it. Bike manufacturers knew a trend when they saw it, and Schwinn came up with the Sting Ray, the first bike built with BMX in mind. (Some people insist it was the birth of the Sting Ray bike that encouraged the growth of BMX and not the other way around. It really doesn't matter. The new bike was destined to change cycling in America forever.)

The Sting Ray bike looked, not surprisingly, just like the famous moto-cross motorcycles of grown-ups. It had smaller wheels (20 inches in diameter), higher handlebars, and a long seat that was soon nicknamed the "banana" seat. Riders found that this new bike was easy to handle, could be turned fast and easy. The ease with which the bike could be handled opened up a new world of tricks, making jumps and turns easier.

The new bike gained in popularity as more and more kids began to use the bike for BMX riding. But they were already beginning to modify the Sting Ray to increase its ruggedness. One of the first of the experimenters was Alan Johnson of Canoga Park, California. He went to his local bicycle shop and asked if a stronger wheel could be built. An active BMX rider, Alan believed the wheels could be made stronger to prevent bent rims. High flying jumps, hard turns, potholes, and other rigors of the tough BMX style were still taking a toll on these bikes.

The First Breakthrough

Russ Okawa, the dealer Alan went to, designed and built a 36-spoke wheel, replacing the customary 28-spoke wheel. This new wheel used a stronger hub as well as more spokes and became the first true BMX wheel. The wheel was thereafter called the "A.J." in honor of the young man who started the new trend.

As more and more Sting Rays were used in BMX races, the manufacturer became swamped with orders to repair broken frames, rims, handlebars, and wheels. To make the bikes stronger, the handlebars were eventually re-designed, making them lower and with a cross brace between the handles for greater stability. Other bike manufacturers began to design and build rugged frames just for bicycle moto-cross.

Southern California, by the way, was the source of nearly 75 percent of the damage claims in the early days of BMX, and Southern California remains the BMX capital of the world.

Tire makers like Goodyear and others jumped into the sport of bicycle moto-cross by designing and making tires with knobby treads, just like the ones used on the motorcycle moto-cross bikes. The grip and digging ability of these tires greatly increased control and, therefore, the excitement of the races.

By the mid-1970s approximately 130,000 moto-cross bikes were racing on over 100 race tracks in California alone. Bicycle moto-cross then erupted across the country, spreading through first the southern states where riding was possible year round, and eventually to every state in the country.

Today's BMX Bike

There have been tremendous changes since the days that Alan Johnson modified his Sting Ray. The BMX bike still uses a standard 20-inch wheel, but little

Bicycle makers finally began to turn out a product that could stand up to the tough competition of BMX racing.

else is the same. BMX bicycles have to be strong to survive the hard pounding of the course. Of equal importance is the weight of the bike. It should be as light as possible—between 18 and 30 pounds, depending upon the age and weight of the rider.

Technology born during the "space age" of the 1960s and '70s is responsible for a lot of improvements. Frames and wheels are no longer plain steel but made instead of lightweight aerospace metals like titanium and aluminum alloys. Some wheels are made from special synthetic plastics or nylons also developed for the B-1 bomber. Handlebars are now chrom-molybdenum or "chrom-moly," a high strength tubing used for aircraft control systems. The seats are no longer steel with foam padding and cloth covers, but are made from strong high-impact plastic.

There have been other improvements. Pedals have raised knobs, chains are stronger, gears and other parts all have been re-engineered with bicycle moto-cross in mind. Tires come in dozens of different tread styles replacing the old knobbys.

Larger cruiser BMX bikes are designed for the heavier weight of older riders.

Cruisers

Cruiser bikes were introduced to bicycle moto-cross because older boys and girls did not want to give up BMX competition simply because they had grown a little older and a little taller.

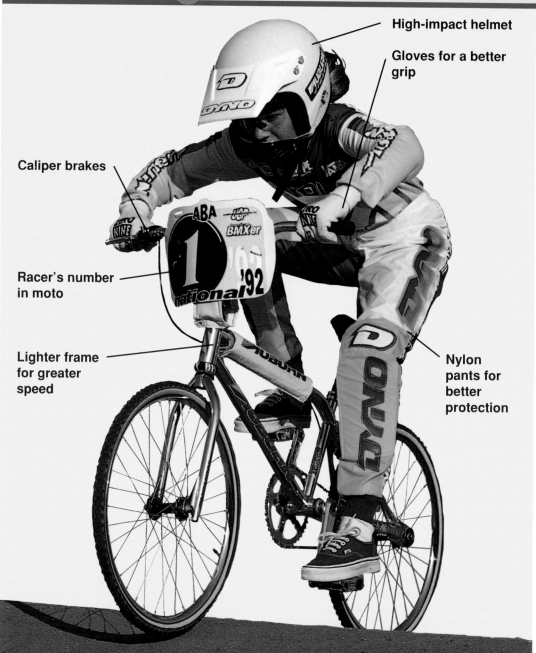

High-impact helmet

Gloves for a better grip

Caliper brakes

Racer's number in moto

Lighter frame for greater speed

Nylon pants for better protection

Safety equipment has also become standard on BMX and Cruiser bikes. The handlebar clamp and upper cross brace on the frame are wrapped in a padded material called "Rad Pads," and the grips are made of soft-molded plastic, improving the rider's ability to hold on. Helmets and goggles for eye protection are mandatory in most BMX-sanctioned races. Nylon trousers, shirts and gloves are now standard for protection during BMX racing.

Cruiser BMX bikes are basically the same as a standard BMX bike except for two important features. The wheels are 24 inches instead of the standard 20-inch wheels. In addition, the cruiser frame is slightly larger and the seat tube is two or more inches longer to accommodate a taller rider.

Like the standard BMX bike, the Cruiser models are constantly improving. For instance, the cruisers now come with an unusual two-speed gear shifter that requires the rider to pedal forward when in low gear, and then pedal backwards to shift into the high-speed second gear! It sounds strange, but many Cruiser riders insist it helps win races! This dual shifting bike is called the American Locomotion Super Cruiser.

Generally the Cruiser bikes race much the same as a standard BMX bike except that the taller bikes make taking tight turns a lot easier because the pedal is higher off the ground. The two-speed shift control makes for a much faster race, too.

They're off—the fence drops to start another BMX moto.

BMX
Competition

Most bicycle moto-cross tracks are dirt, ranging between one-eighth of a mile to a full quarter-mile long. Indoor tracks are shorter, requiring a minimum of 15,000 to 20,000 square feet of area. These limitations do not dampen the spirit of the races, however. In fact, the shorter tracks encourage tighter turns with higher banked dirt berms, increasing the excitement of each race. Since each race is shorter and faster, the combination creates an atmosphere of high tension as each racer struggles to gain the most out of the short track.

Out of necessity, most indoor races are held in stadiums normally used for athletic events like football or basketball. Indoor tracks are usually dirt, but in some cases smaller tracks may be built on slick concrete floors with resin placed on the floor at the turns to make tighter turns possible. Carpeted, wooden ramps are sometimes built for indoor use, but are not recommended by the BMX racing organizations. Wood is more likely to cause injury when a spill occurs.

BMX races can be held both indoors and outdoors. The indoor racing tracks are often built in the middle of athletic arenas.

Whether indoors or outdoors, all BMX tracks are built for safety as well as excitement. The starting line should have enough room for eight to ten bikes and riders to line up side-by-side across the starting point.

Each moto or racing heat consists of eight to ten riders, and is started by a flag man with an elastic line stretched across the front of the riders and then released. Many tracks have "European style" starting fences where each rider rests his front tire against the fence. When the fence is dropped, the race begins.

The course is built with mounds of varying elevations. Uphill climbs are always gentle, but downhill runs can be steep. All turns must have a berm or barrier on the outside of the turn, allowing the rider to maintain control in a high speed turn.

Some turns are sharp, but they can still be taken at high speed. The most difficult high speed turn is always a left-hand turn because the chain sprocket of a BMX bike is on the right side. This keeps the sprocket and chain out of the dirt as riders lean into each left-hand turn. The track is designed so that a rider will be able to pass another in a turn. This means that high speed turns must be at least 10 to 15 feet wide, and slow turns at least 6 feet wide.

Straightaways are 10 to 15 feet wide. The longest straightaway usually includes a jump of at least three feet. The next longest straightaway will have a series of mounds called *whoop-de-dos*, approximately one-foot high and 10 to 15 feet apart. Many tracks, especially outdoor ones, put mud holes immediately after each jump—no doubt to encourage the rider to go for distance if he wants to avoid a mushy landing!

All solid objects around the course such as poles, boulders, fences, and trees are padded to prevent injury. Potholes should be shallow, and ditches caused by rain runoff should be leveled before each event.

The Race

Before each race you and some of the riders will walk the course, much the same as motorcycle and auto race drivers do. You do this to learn as much as possible about the layout of each track. Experience has taught you that each track is different from location to location.

Points are awarded after each moto. Most BMX racers collect points from race to race, striving to eventually qualify for Regional or even National races. National races occur about four times each year. In order to qualify for points, the race must be approved by the National Bicycle League or the U.S. Cycling Federation. The race must also occur on an approved track. Some serious riders will race in unapproved events to build experience and skill, even though they earn no points.

To win any BMX race a rider has to keep his wheels in contact with the track as much as possible, and that means keeping your airborne leaps as low as possible.

Tactical Tips

Bicycle moto-cross is unlike most types of racing. Your speed is not constant, varying as each obstacle is met and each turn is made. The following tips may help you improve your race.

Concentration. Focus totally on where you and your bike are in the race at all times. Mentally track every foot of the course as you approach each new spot, planning ahead for what is coming, ready to react to what's around you. Only think of your race and your ride, not the rider next to you.

Contact. Whoop-de-dos and other obstacles are made to push your bike up and off the track to slow you down. Always strive to keep your rear tire on the ground as much as possible. Jumps are critical. If the jump is low you can pull up the front wheel and do a *wheelie* over the mound, keeping the rear tire in contact with the track surface while the front tire rises naturally.

In the case of *table-tops*, you may find yourself airborne with no choice. Just get your bike on the ground as quickly as possible; driving, not leaping, will get you to the finish line faster. Or, as BMX riders like to say, "In the air for show, on the ground for go!"

If you must go airborne remember this: You and your bike are not accelerating, you are decelerating. Your rear wheel is not on the ground and driving, and your front wheel offers no steering control.

Landing. Always land with the rear tire first, then gently lower the front tire. If you land on the front tire you can easily lose control and—boom—you're out of the race by pulling a major endo.

Look forward. Never turn to look behind. This will break your concentration and serves no purpose during the race. The distraction will cause you to slow down. You do not want to do this. Looking back may also cause you to miss a turn or tumble into a bike and rider that have just taken a spill in front of you. So remember, the rider behind you is not important.

Turns. When you enter a turn, try to delay braking as long as possible while maintaining control and driving the rear wheel. The turn is where many inexperienced riders will slack up! But you must be aggressive in order to leap ahead in each turn. Never allow another rider into a turn as long as you can safely enter the turn first. This is for two reasons: First, you cannot pass a rider tracking along the same line as you are; second (and equally important), bikes behind you are safe. However, the bike in front of you may endo, taking you with him.

It is possible to pass in front of another bike in a turn without cutting off the other rider. Try to maintain at least one bike length in front as you cut past him to either side of the turn. Do not enter the turn recklessly. You will be disqualified.

Keep your weight equally on both the front and back wheels while in the turn. A common beginner's mistake is to allow the front wheel to float, losing

Turns are a critical part of the BMX race, where opposing riders try to stay in front of you to prevent you from passing.

traction. No traction, no control. Lastly, in the turn always remember to keep the inside pedal up. If you don't, it may dig into the ground and then your race is over.

Freestyle Riding

During many BMX events across the country many riders entertain the crowds between motos with exhibitions of stunt riding and tricks. Most experienced BMX riders have no problem learning some freestyle stunts.

Most riders start out with a bike that has the standard coaster brakes, which are applied by reversing the direction of the pedals and pushing backward. This motion, as any bike rider knows, causes the rear wheel brake to tighten. The harder you apply backward pressure, the more braking action you get, until the brake locks up. A BMX bike has caliper brakes similar to those on a 10-speed bike. An experienced BMX rider has commonly spent thousands of hours learn-

SIDEHACKS

Sidehacks are special BMX bikes that are built to carry a passenger called the *monkey*. Sidehacks are just like their motorcycle cousins, the sidecar. The driver and his co-rider work together to ride their way to victory.

Sidehack bikes carry twice the weight of the standard BMX bike and must be built very strong. Yet keeping the weight down is as important to sidehack racing as it is in standard or cruiser BMX racing. Weight slows the racer down in any sport.

The width of the sidehack is important, and is customized to fit the team members. If the rig is too wide, the bike and sidehack will not track well, and the driver will end up dragging the sidehack around the course. If the rig is too narrow, the monkey will not have enough room to move around. The co-rider and the driver must both be aware of their balance as they shift their weight from side to side during the race.

ing how to use these hand operated brakes for racing.

It may sound like a simple skill, but the BMX rider has to develop a second, completely different level of riding skills to manage freestyle stunt techniques. Many of these stunts are easy. Most require a great deal of practice and considerable athletic ability. Here are just a few:

Wheelie. Yes, this is the same technique used by seasoned BMX racers to navigate bumps, table-tops, and other BMX obstacles. The freestyle stunt rider will not only go up on his back wheel, but stay there as long as he wants.

Kickturn. Here, the rider climbs a mound until he just barely reaches the top. He then jerks the handlebars backward, stopping the forward motion of his bike. At the same time he twists his body, pulling the handlebars with him to complete a 180-degree turn. The rider is now facing down the mound.

Pogo. The pogo is a sort of bouncing wheelie. The rider balances on the axle of either wheel, letting his weight lift the other wheel off the ground, then jerks upward carrying the rest of the bike up with him. He repeats this over and over, bouncing on his two-wheeler as if on a pogo stick.

Sidewalk. Here's where the rider first balances on the pedals, his bike at a standstill. The rider then pulls the bike up sideways and drops the front wheel down 90 degrees in a new direction. Next, the rider flips the back wheel up and goes further in that direction, flopping the front and back wheels back and forth like a sidewinder rattlesnake—the bike is moving sideways. Both the pogo and sidewalk require lots of practice and upper arm strength.

Bunnyhops. Bunnyhops allow the rider to jump over obstacles. The rider begins a standard wheelie and when the front tire clears the center of the obstacle he pushes forward on the handlebars and "flicks" the back wheel up at the same time! The world record bunnyhop is a jump over an obstacle 46 inches high.

Barhop. The barhop requires great balance. Riding at a speed great enough to maintain balance, the rider hops up to the center bar of the frame and scoots up to the handlebars. Next, the rider brings the knees up to the handlebars to stand on the cross brace. The rider is now squatting on the bar brace over the front tire. Being careful not to shift too far forward, the rider extends the legs forward to end up sitting on the cross bar with legs stretched out forward over the front wheel!

If you can master a BMX bike to successfully perform some of these tricks, then racing may be a breeze!

Freestyle BMX riders are trying all sorts of new stunts, including riding some specially designed bikes over rugged obstacle courses.

Cross-country road racing is as popular as cross-country running, but cyclists usually race over much longer distances.

Road Racing

Sooner or later, it had to happen. Cyclists would want to compete on the open road, just like automobile drivers do in certain competitions called Grand Prix racing. The challenge of riding across and through natural open areas as well as cities and towns is what riding a bicycle is all about. Many road races cover hundreds of miles and feature hundreds of competitors, too. Courses in some of the longer road races can stretch for miles, with different age groups competing at the same time for finishing places in their category. Even disabled persons who race in customized three-wheel vehicles using only their arms for pedal power compete in amateur road races.

Mountain biking is the new recreational sport that takes riders over natural trails once reserved just for hikers and backpackers.

There are other bicycle challenges, too. Off road racing that literally leaves the pavement behind has become enormously popular, especially in North America. Those who take to trails in our mountains and canyons aren't always racing—many do it to enjoy the sights, smells, and sounds of nature, just as backpackers and hikers do. This new form of sport and recreation is called mountain cycling.

Modern American mountain biking began just a few years ago in Marin County, California. Up until this time there were only two types of off road bikes. The first was the enormously popular BMX bike. The second type of bike was the light European Cyclo cross bike, relatively unknown in the United States.

BMX bikes were rejected for mountain cycling because of their size. Most riders looking for cross country trail riding were adults. The European Cyclo cross bikes were expensive and had narrow tires and drop handle bars. These bikes were difficult to ride and were more like high spirited road racing bikes than a bike that could handle the stress of cross country biking.

The cyclists of Marin County began to build their own version of the European Cyclo cross—a totally new type of off road bike. The new bike retained the fat knobby tires and basic frame of the BMX bike. Then the designers borrowed the cantilever braking system found on the Cyclo cross bikes. Next they took the derailers and top of the line components from racing bikes, and the efficient multi-gear drive trains found on touring bikes.

The final change was a second look at the BMX frame. They changed the geometry to a more upright style, placing the rider and the pedals higher off the ground. The end result: the modern trail or mountain bike.

Mountain bikers love to get away from it all.

Cyclists have taken their mountain bikes everywhere. The sport has spread worldwide. Mountain bike racing is found on all types of terrain and in all types of weather. There is one drawback to owning a mountain bike, however. When you ride a lot along regular paved roads on a mountain bike, riding is not as easy as it would be with a touring bike. That's why most mountain cyclists have at least two bikes, so they can continue to ride when they are not on a trail in the wilderness.

Cyclo cross

In Europe, the Cyclo cross bike is considered to be the original cross country off road bike. Cyclo cross was developed in France in the late 1940s when riders were looking for a way to stay in shape during the wintertime. Road racing and touring are nearly impossible in the harsher winters of Europe.

The Cyclo cross bike looks like a standard 10-speed bike except it has no fenders and fat tires. The European bikes still retain the drop down handlebars of the road bike. Like their American cousins, these bicycles are also very light and have gear drive trains adapted from road racing technology.

Cyclo cross races are short and intense. They last about an hour, although individual course conditions can slow down riders. Typically, Europe is wet and muddy in the winter. Cyclo cross events find riders traveling through small forests, up steep hills, and down muddy ravines. Many riders end up carrying their bikes at a dead run along parts of the course to reach the finish line.

Cyclo cross is a major cycling sport in Europe today. Many riders prefer the short difficult races over the popular six-day road races. Oddly enough, there are fewer injuries on off road races than occur on road races!

Road Racing

As the name suggests, road racing takes place on paved roads. Most races occur on roads normally used for public transportation, but sometimes an entire course may be built just for the race.

The 1977 Tour of Italy caused officials to construct special planks to span the canals of Venice, Italy. During the 1980 Moscow Olympic Games, the entire road race was held on a circuit built especially for that race!

Road racing itself is simple. The circuit is clearly laid out and marked. A group of riders start at the sound of the starter's pistol. The first rider across the finish line is declared the winner! What makes road racing a challenge is the

A typical circuit race can involve hundreds of riders, some competing in different age categories.

design of the circuit or race course. The course may be short, requiring the riders to complete several laps to cover the required distance. The course may also be long—up to several hundred miles long, requiring much endurance from the road racer.

Most amateur circuit road races in North America can be up to 80 miles long. Women race about 40 miles; junior men about 50 miles; and the seniors race from 60- to 80-mile circuits.

The Road Racing Bicycle

The bicycles used by road racers resemble simple 10-speed bikes, common everywhere in North America and Europe. In fact, the 10-speed bike is eligible for competition in amateur classes, especially for beginning riders.

As each rider moves up in experience, the sophistication of his or her bike increases. Road bikes enjoy the same technological advantages all other racing and riding bikes have. Choosing the right bicycle depends on the rider's experience and body type, as well as the type of event. For example, bikes used by the professional or serious amateur are usually chosen for their light weight. Different drive trains are chosen to fit the specific race. Simply put, there is no single road bike that's right for all riders and all races. There are thousands to choose from, ranging from the least expensive 10-speed to a deluxe 20-speed graphite bike made specifically for the Tour de France.

Many disabled people love to compete in circuit cycling races.

Point to Point Races

Circuit races are common in America because they are easier to organize than point to point races. The longer the point to point race, the more reluctant authorities are to close public highways for hours on end as the event proceeds. Shorter circuit races only require road closures for a few minutes at key intersections if the race is timed and run properly. Point to point races in America are much shorter and less dangerous than some of those run throughout Europe.

Point to point races are a challenge to riders because they rarely have the opportunity to learn the many hazards and difficulties along the way starting out. International amateur point to point races are between 110 and 120 miles; professional races are 150 to 190 miles in length. These races are no place for inexperienced riders.

Many riders will attempt a long distance point to point race three or more times before they even successfully finish the race. That's right—they enter but rarely finish their first time.

Experienced point to point riders list the Paris Roubaix race as the world's most difficult to complete, let alone win. The course runs 165 miles as it winds through northern France. The worst part is that at least 40 miles of the Paris Roubaix course is over bone jarring, bike thrashing cobblestones!

Criteriums

The shortest circuit races are called *criteriums.* These races are flat, extremely short courses that come close to track racing. These race courses are

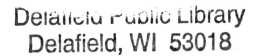

generally no longer than a mile and a half. It is no surprise that the best criterium racers have a great deal of experience racing on high-banked tracks. Track racers cannot make a simple switch to road racing. They must develop those skills necessary to compete on rough, uneven public roads. Other criteriums have extreme hill circuits favoring riders who have a great deal of off road experience such as mountain biking, Cyclo cross, or bicycle moto-cross!

Stage Races

Probably the most famous of road races remains the Tour de France. This race covers over 2,300 miles and takes at least three weeks to complete. The Tour de France is an example of a stage race. Stage races are popular in Europe. The rider who tackles this kind of race must be in top physical condition. After hundreds of miles in all kinds of weather, most riders fail. These riders continue to try again and again building their stamina until they can just finish, and someday hope to win.

The world's premier road racer of the past decade has to be the incredible Greg LeMond. Greg became the first American to win the prestigious Tour de France. Greg has won this race an unbelievable three times!

Oddly enough, Greg's first love of sports centered around skiing, no doubt because his father was an avid skier. Once while he prepared to attend a ski camp as a young man, Greg witnessed the Nevada State cycling championships. This race was hard to miss as part of the course went right past the front of his house.

Greg could see that the sport required great physical capabilities, and so Greg resolved to get into cycling as a way to stay in shape for skiing during the off season. Greg's whole family is into sports. His younger sister Karen won the 1977 Amateur Athletic Union National Championship in gymnastics as a member of the U.S. gymnastics team.

At age fourteen, Greg won the very first race he entered in Sacramento, California. The race was a criterium circuit race where Greg competed in the 13- to 15-year-old class. The very next day he won his second race in Dublin California, the famous Tassajara road race. This is one of the few races that allows the younger "intermediate" class (13- to 15-year-olds). The race was a rugged, point to point race 18 miles long. Interestingly, Greg's father competed in the same race in the senior category.

Greg's first major race was the Tour de Fresno in 1977. To everyone's amazement, he finished only seconds behind first-place winner John Howard, a

Greg LeMond is one of the best cyclists in the world, winning the world famous Tour de France a remarkable three times.

great cyclist. Greg was still competing in the junior category! Greg had arrived in the sport of cycling, and was known in racing circles as "the phenom from Nevada." Greg went on to win the Junior World's Championship in 1978, and set his sights on the 1980 Olympics. Unfortunately, Greg was not able to compete in the Olympics that year because the United States boycotted the host country, the former Soviet Union.

Greg LeMond was introduced to European racing in 1980 as a member of the United States National team. The race was the Circuit de la Sarth, one of the few races open to both professional and amateur racers. Greg stunned the European racing community by becoming the first American—in fact, the youngest of any nationality, professional or amateur—to win a major stage race in the history of the sport.

LeMond eventually signed a contract with the Renault team of France and began his professional career, winning his first professional race at the Tour de l'Oise. In 1981, his first major victory occurred not in Europe, but in America. Greg won the Coors Classic, a pro-am race, beating Olympic champion Sergei Soukhorouchenkow, a famous Soviet racer.

In 1982, Greg went on to win the Tour de Avenir, the pro-am version of the Tour de France. This was the first time he had totally dominated the race as a professional, with an incredible 10-minute spread at the finish. More victories followed, including the World Championship in 1983 and the Tour de France in 1985. Greg LeMond's record is impossibly long, and he has become a legend in cycling.

Time Trials

Time trial racing is probably the most physically and mentally intense of road racing events. The reason is that each rider is competing against both the clock for time and against other riders. Riders set off alone at spaced intervals to face the road alone.

Because time trial contestants have no other riders that they can draft, their racing time is "pure." *Drafting* in road racing is a technique of alternately changing places with the rider in front. It takes a great deal of effort to cut through the air if you are the front racer. Riders immediately behind you will find the riding easier. When teams ride together, team members will switch from the front position to the rear so they get a chance to rest during a race. If you can draft behind an opponent, so much the better. He does the work while you travel the same number of miles with him in relative ease.

On a time trial, the contestant is always the lead rider. In America the most common time trial is 25 miles "out and back"; that is, 12.5 miles per leg. In Europe, time trials tend to be more diverse and courses vary over many distances. The most famous is the Grand Prix de Nations. This race is 45 miles long and is considered to be both difficult and dangerous by many professional riders.

The most common amateur team time trial race is the four-man, 64-mile race. Team time trials also are held in the Olympic Games. In 1984, the U.S. team won a bronze medal.

This team entered in Delaware's Tour Du Pont goes for it in a grueling time trial.

Velodrome racing is a fast-paced sport where spectators can enjoy the events from start to finish.

Track Racing

CHAPTER FIVE

Bicycle track racing began in North America in 1893. The place was the first World Cycling Championship held in Chicago, Illinois. It was unusual that the first event of its kind should be held in North America, because at that time Europe was the undisputed cycling capital of the world, with many cycling tracks. Maybe it was because American cyclists were in demand all over the world. Some professional cyclists earned up to an unheard of $1,000 per day. By the 1920s, bicycle track racing became one of the world's most popular indoor sports, often drawing crowds of more than 20,000 people.

Just as some things come into and then go out of popularity, indoor cycling began to fade in the 1930s and 1940s due to World War II. It was not until the 1960s that cycling increased in popularity. Today, there are 19 first-class velodromes in the United States.

Velodrome racing is perhaps more exciting for spectators than road racing, because the crowd can see the entire race from their seats. Their eyes are kept glued to the track as men and women compete individually and in teams in time trials and pursuits.

The oval-shaped track used in indoor bicycle racing is called a *velodrome*. Velodromes can be built outdoors as well. The surface of the track can by made of wood, asphalt, or concrete. Grass and dirt velodromes are rare, and seldom used any longer. Wood is the fastest race track surface, but is most commonly used inside, while concrete is preferred outdoors.

All velodromes, no matter where they are built, look the same. The track has two straights or straightaways. These are linked by two curved sections. Because the races are run in a counterclockwise direction, all turns are to the left. The entire track is banked, providing a slope that makes racing around such a tight course easier. If the entire course were flat, the race would have to be run much more slowly. The highest tilt or maximum banking occurs at each end. The straightaways are also banked, but only half as much as the turns.

The area in the center of the track is called the *infield*. This area is used as a warm up area for the cyclists and has seating for coaches, officials, and others who may be helping out at the race. The infield is also used as an emergency run off in the event of an accident or other emergency. Around the infield is an area called the apron. The riders use this area to mount their bikes and enter the track. Surrounding the velodrome is a fence or railing. Beyond the railing is seating for the spectators.

Painted on the track itself are several lines. It's confusing at first, because there are so many and they are employed for different racing events. The first is the *pole line*. This is the line nearest to the apron and infield. It is used to measure the official length of the track. Seventy centimeters up from the pole line is the sprinter's line. This line and all others are parallel to the pole line. The area between the pole line and the sprinter's line is called the pole. The pole is an area used in sprint events. Halfway up the track is another parallel line called the stayer's line.

No sprint seems faster or more exhausting than the sprints in cycling.

The size of each track is different. The largest outdoor velodromes are between 400 and 500 meters around. At 400 meters, the track is roughly one-quarter of a mile long. The minimum track length for any outdoor world championship event is 333-1/3 meters. Indoor velodromes are much smaller. A track 285 meters around would be considered large for an indoor track. Most indoor velodromes measure only 200 meters. Many are smaller still, even down to 130 meters.

Many wooden velodrome tracks are portable, making many large stadiums and indoor arenas suitable for indoor bike racing events. Even though your city may not have a velodrome of its own, don't be surprised if one day you go to a bike race where just the week before you saw a professional basketball game!

The Competitors

To be a top sprinting cyclist, Olympic-style, you need to have two things above all else: single-minded attention on your goal and a lot of stamina. Sprinters who race the clock around the velodrome track have learned to focus all their effort into improving their elapsed time by thousandths of a second.

Races are of varying lengths, and have different names like matched sprints, pursuits, road race, and so on. The individual pursuit and the team pursuit are both exciting events where elapsed time does not determine who ultimately wins. In the elimination heats (quarterfinals, semifinals) the winner of each heat is whoever crosses the finish line first. Eventually, four riders (or four teams) are left who compete one pair at a time. It's possible for the bronze medalist to have a faster heat than the silver or gold medalist did in theirs.

What makes pursuit more fun to watch is the way the race is run. Each rider (or team) begins at opposite ends of the track (that is, your competition starts one-half lap distant from where you start). Your opponent (or the opposing team, if a four-man pursuit) is racing the clock, but if the other rider catches up and passes you before the heat is over, they automatically win.

In matched sprints, two riders race three times around the track. At first, however, they don't exactly look like they're racing. They look like they're riding at a snail's pace. The riders play a game of chicken, each one just pacing the other and not pedalling full speed, waiting for the opponent to make a break for the finish line. When one of the riders finally takes off to sprint, the other one can draft behind the lead rider to take advantage of his windbreak. Sometimes the gamble pays off and the lead rider tires just enough for the second rider to pass and win. Other times, the second rider waits a fraction of a second too long to go in pursuit, and the lead rider wins.

The first American to medal in the Olympic one-kilometer track sprint was Erin Hartwell, who had only been in training six years when he took the bronze with a time of 64.753 seconds—good enough to beat some of the best riders in the world. Imagine a race where you have no opponents alongside of you—just yourself and the clock ticking away. The one-kilometer sprint is a four-lap race of all-out exertion, and with no opponent to egg you on, it takes grit and determination to fly around the track. At the Barcelona Games in 1992, Hartwell had it.

"Every dream came true for me at that moment," Hartwell remembers.

Women cyclists did not compete in the Olympics until the 1984 games in Los Angeles. It was appropriate, then, that the gold and silver medalists that year in the women's individual road race were Americans Connie Carpenter and Rebecca Twigg.

Riders in a team pursuit take turns cycling at the front, drafting for their teammates.

That same year, American Mark Gorski was an underdog because he was coming back from a serious cycling injury in 1981. But Gorski beat the odds and took the gold medal in match sprints.

Track Racing Bicycles

The track racing bicycle can be described in one word: simple. A velodrome bicycle is stripped down to its most basic parts. None of the complicated gears and braking systems, fenders, tire pumps or other items commonly used on road, off road, or BMX cycles are on a track bike.

A track bike's drive train is a direct drive device; it has only one fixed gear. This means the bike has no brakes for stopping, no freewheel ability for coasting, no derailer, and no gear shifting mechanism of any kind. As a result, the bikes are very light and fast. The average track bike weighs in at just 28 pounds!

A direct drive train means that your speed is controlled entirely with the pedals. To go faster, the rider has to pump or pedal faster. To slow down a little, the rider rests and lets the momentum lift his legs up and down with the pedals. There is no braking system.

The frame of the track bike is designed especially for use on steep banked tracks; it is more upright or taller than most bikes. This allows for maximum pedal length without the rider colliding with the track during a power stroke. The frame is also designed with a much shorter wheelbase, minimizing the distance between wheels for greater control.

Track bikes are actually safer than touring or off road bikes because of the shape of the track. Brakes are not used on these bikes because they are not needed. All the riders are going in the same direction and on the same enclosed track. Brakes on a track bike would actually be dangerous to use and cause mishaps. Controlling one's speed directly through the pedals is safer and faster than having to reach for a hand brake on the handlebars.

Track riders do need to change gears now and then, but the rider must remove the rear tire and pedals. The individual cog is changed for one the rider feels is more suited to the specific race. (A cog is the metal wheel with teeth that threads through the chain and turns the wheel when the pedals are pushed.)

Gear changes depend upon the surface of the track, how steeply the track is banked, whether contestants are racing indoors or outdoors, and the length of the race. Choosing the right gear is important, because once the rider has decided, he can't change gears during the race.

Some of the addresses below are where you may write for more information; they are not always the same as the actual street addresses of the velodrome in that city.

Alkek Velodrome
City of Houston Parks &
  Recreation Dept.
18203 Groeschke
Houston, TX 77084

Alpenrose Velodrome
4318 SE 8th Court
Gresham, OR 97080

Baton Rouge Velodrome
E. Baton Rouge Parks &
  Recreation
P.O. Box 15887
Baton Rouge, LA 70895

Dick Lane Velodrome
1431 Norman Berry Dr.
East Point, GA 30344

Dorias Velodrome
P.O. Box 63
Royal Oak, MI 48068

Encino Velodrome
P.O. Box 16006
Encino, CA 91416

Hellyer Park Velodrome
385 Hellyer Ave.
San Jose, CA 95111

Kissena Velodrome
44 Clifford St.
Lynnbrook, NY 11563

Lehigh County Velodrome
217 Main St.
Emmaus, PA 18049

Major Taylor Velodrome
3649 Cold Spring Rd.
Indianapolis, IN 46222

Marymoor Velodrome
4710 University Way NE
Seattle, WA 98105

National Sports Center
  Velodrome
1700 105th Ave. NE
Blaine, MN 55434

Olympic Velodrome
CSU Dominguez Hills
1000 E. Victoria
Carson, CA 90747

Brian Piccolo Park Velodrome
9501 Sheridan St.
Cooper City, FL 33024

Edward Rudolph Meadowhill
  Velodrome
Northbrook Park District
111 Waukegan Rd.
Northbrook, IL 60062

St. Louis Velodrome
  Association
1550 Eastham
St. Louis, MO 63146

San Diego Velodrome
2221 Morley Field Dr.
San Diego, CA 92104

7-Eleven Velodrome
U.S. Olympic Committee
One Olympic Plaza
Colorado Springs, CO 80909

Washington Park Bowl
P.O. Box 836
Kenosha, WI 53141

Bicycle track racing events are planned and scheduled by bicycle clubs, individual sponsors and, in some cases, regional and state committees. The United States Cycling Federation (USCF) is the governing body of both amateur and professional track race events in the U.S.

The USCF sanctions, or gives approval to, individual racing events; licenses individual racers; approves new track and bicycle designs; and conducts the U.S. National Championships. The USCF also selects the cycling teams that compete in the World Championships, the Olympic Games, and other important international events.

Today's track racing cycles are designed to get the best aerodynamic results.

Bringing It Home

In 1996 the Olympic Games will be held in Atlanta, Georgia, and it should be an exciting time for American cyclists. Those competitors from around the United States who perform the best at various national and international meets during the previous year will be invited to tryout for the Olympic cycling team. They will be facing many great riders from around the world, especially from Europe and Australia. Their hard work and competitive spirit will be their greatest allies as they bicycle their way to untold glories.

Glossary

Apron. Starting point in indoor race track.

Barhop. BMX stunt where rider rides on crossbar of handlebars.

BMX. Bicycle moto-cross.

Bunnyhop. Stunt to propel rider over bumps and obstacles.

Caliper. A type of brake that applies pressure to either side of a bicycle wheel, controlled with levers on the handlebars.

Cog. Metal wheel with teeth, part of a bicycle's drive train.

Criterium. Shortest circuit road race.

Cruiser. Type of BMX bike (24 inches vs. standard 20 inches).

Cyclo cross. Original European off-road race.

Draft. The art of resting behind the lead rider in a race.

Float. When the front wheel loses traction.

Heat. Single racing event.

Infield. Center area of an indoor track.

Knobby. Type of BMX racing tire.

Kickturn. Stunt where rider "kicks" his bike into the opposite direction.

Moto. Group of eight to ten riders. Also, a "heat."

Monkey. Nickname of sidehack co-driver.

Pole line. Line between infield and course of indoor track.

Pogo. Stunt where rider makes illusion of pogo stick.

Rad pad. Foam safety pads on BMX bikes.

Sidehack. Special two-man BMX bike.

Table-top. Series of flat topped bumps.

Wheelie. Stunt where rider rides on rear wheel only.

Whoop-de-dos. Series of foot-high bumps.

For Additional Information

There are many interesting books you may read about cycling, and many cycling clubs and associations throughout North America. Some of them are listed below.

Better BMX Riding & Racing by George Sullivan. New York, NY: Dodd, Mead, 1983.

Bicycle Motocross by Jack Scagnetti. Vancouver, BC: Clark, Irwin & Co. Ltd., 1976.

Bicycle Rider by Mary Scioscia. New York, NY: Harper & Row, 1983.

Bicycle Road Racing by Barbara George. Don Mills, Ontario: J. M. Dent & Sons Ltd., 1977.

Bicycle Track Racing by Barbara George. Don Mills, Ontario: J. M. Dent & Sons Ltd., 1977.

Bicycle Touring by the Editors of Bicycling Magazine. Emmaus, PA: Rondale Press, 1985.

Bicycle Touring by Peter Mohn. Mankato, MN: Crestwood House, 1975.

Bicyling Clubs:

Bikecentinnial, P.O. Box 8308, Missoula, MT 59807.

League of American Wheelmen, 190 W. Ostend St., Ste. 120, Baltimore, MD 21230.

Bicyclists of Iowa City, P.O. Box 846, Iowa City, IA 5240.

Bloomington Bicycle Club, P.O. Box 463, Bloomington IN 47402.

California Association of Bicycling Organizations (CABO), P.O. Box 2684, Dublin, CA 94568.

Cascade Bicycle Club, P.O. Box 31299, Seattle, WA 98103.

Charles River Wheelmen, 19 Chase Ave., West Newton, MA 02165.

Concerned Off-Road Bicycle Association (CORBA), 15236 Victory Blvd., Box 149, Van Nuys, CA 91411.

Denver Bicycle Touring Club, Box 9873, Denver CO 80201.

Florida Bicycle Association, c/o 210 Lake Hollingsworth, #1707, Lakeland, FL 33803.

Granite State Wheelmen, 16 Clinton St., Salem NH 03079.

Greater Arizona Bicycling Association (GABA), Phoenix Chapter,
    P.O. Box 9308, Tempe, AZ 85281.
Grizzly Peak Cyclists, P.O.Box 9308, Berkeley, CA 94709.
Los Angeles Wheelmen, 2212 Chamwood Ave., Alhambra, CA 91803.
Louisville Wheelmen, P.O. Box 35541, Louisville, KY 40232.
Ohio Bicycle Federation, 9611 Lorain Ave., Cleveland, OH 44102.
Potomac Pedalers, P.O. Box 23601, L'Enfant Plaza Station, Washington, D.C.
    20024.
Washington Area Bicyclist Association (WABA), 1819 H. St. NW, Ste. 640,
    Washington D.C. 20006.

Bicycling Organizations:

American Bicycle Association (ABA), P.O. Box 714, Chandler, AZ. BMX races.
Bay Area Ridge Trail Council, 116 New Montgomery, Ste. 640,
    San Francisco, CA 94105. Bay Area trail system.
Bicycle Federation of America, 1818 R St. NW, Washington D.C. 20009.
    Publish *Pro Bike News.*
Bicycle Helmet Safety Institute, 4611 Seventh St., South Arlington, VA 22204.
The Bicycle Network, P.O. Box 8194, Philadelphia, PA 19109.
    Publish *The Network News,* a bicycle news clipping service.
Canadian Cycling Association, 1600 James Naismith Dr., Gloucester, Ontario
    K1B 5N4 Canada.
International Mountain Biking Association, P.O. Box 412043, Los Angeles,
    CA 90041.
International Randonneurs, 7272 N. Salina St., Syracuse, NY 13224.
    Paris-Brest-Paris Marathon ride sponsors.
League of American Wheelmen (LAW), 190 W. Ostend St., Ste. 120,
    Baltimore, MD Publish *Bicycle USA.*
National Bicycle Center, P.O. Box 3401, Redmond, WA 98073.
National Bicycle League, 211 Brandenton Ave., Ste. 100, Dublin, OH 43017.
    Sanctioning organization for BMX and freestyle racing.
Ultra Marathon Cycling Association, 2761 N. Marengo Ave., Altadena, CA
    91001. Promotes long distance races.
U.S. Cycling Federation, 1750 E. Boulder St., Colorado Springs, CO 80909.
    Directs U.S. amateur racing.
U.S. Professional Cycling Association, Rt. 1, Box 1650, New Tripoli, PA
    18066. Governs professional cycling.
Women's Cycling Coalition, P.O. Box 281, Louisville, CO 80027.

Index